To: Sis C
From: D.J. Hunter
David Hunter Jr.

PEN IN MY HAND

By
David Hunter Jr.

Thank you for all of your love and support! Love you!!

Copyright © 2013 David Hunter Jr.
All rights reserved.

ISBN: 0615782949
ISBN 13: 9780615782942

Library of Congress Control Number: 2013904502
David Hunter Jr, Los Angeles, CA

FOREWORD

It is with sheer excitement, anticipation, and delight that I endorse and sanction the poetic expressions of David Hunter, Jr., in *Pen In My Hand*. My first encounter with David was linked to his passion and professional pursuit as an actor. I was serving in the role of his casting director and playwright of my award-winning stage play, *A Change Is Gonna Come*. Impressed with his professionalism, "cool" demeanor, and outstanding showmanship in the role of the defense attorney, I submitted David in the category of "Best Supporting Actor" to the prestigious Velocity Magazine Awards, in Washington DC, which he, without question—WON! Now David has expanded his talents and broadened his professional portfolio to include—published author, which I am equally impressed and extremely proud.

The title, *Pen In My Hand*, emphasizes the power of the written word—lives have been dramatically changed; nations have been historically and geographically transformed; empires have been genetically restructured; with one "stroke of a pen". I envision David's compilation of heart-felt poetic masterwork will have a synonymous affect, also. Furthermore, I am optimistic that ardent readers will be equally delighted to gain insightful pleasure in the unique stanzas that David has so passionately composed and chosen to share with us for inspiration, for years to come! Touché, my friend! A job well done!

Vickie L. Evans – National Best-selling Author and Award-winning Director/Playwright– www.forgiven2.com

PREFACE

The title of this book, "Pen In My Hand", was taken from the first poem that I wrote upon moving to Los Angeles, California. As I've grown over the years, I thank God for giving me the outlet of not only being an Actor, but also the creative ability to paint my life story with a pen as I write poetry.

I started writing poetry during my sophomore year of high school to pass the time and get through the day, while also trying to entertain my classmates. Nowadays, writing poetry gives me the time to think about my life and all that has transpired to make me who I am today.

The collection of poems along with two short stories (A Special Bond and Forever Yours) in this book are very personal to me but I am more than happy to invite readers, such as you, into my life, heart and mind; sharing with you many of my very own life experiences. Most of these experiences took place with friends while a few poems were inspired from my friends and their own situations. All of these stories combined helped make "Pen In My Hand" what it is today.

Many of you have asked me why I delayed the release of my book and I want to give the answer to that question. Previously, "Pen in My Hand" was due to be released during the fall of 2011. This all changed when I became ill during the summer of 2011. It started off as just something I thought was minor but after 5 months of back and forth hospital trips and still not knowing what was wrong, there was no other choice but to push everything back.

From the month of July until late September I was painfully ill. I lost 40lbs during this time and was told that I had an allergic reaction/infection in my dietary system and in my liver. Later, I was diagnosed with Celiacs Disease; meaning that I would need to make a complete lifestyle change in the foods that I allowed to enter my body. Having rarely been sick for much of all my life, this was very discouraging. There were days when I felt like

I would not make it through because of the physical pain I was in. There were also days when the mental battle became so intense and all I could do was cry. *Why me? Why was this happening? What did I do?* These questions popped in and out of my head every second of every moment while I was experiencing these tough times.

It truly was the Grace of God that kept me! The abundance of love and comfort that was shown by family and friends during this time is something that I will always cherish. Without this show of affection I do not believe that I would have been able to make it. I was reminded by my Faith in God that He knows the plans that He has for me (Jeremiah 29:11) and even though I didn't have the answer as to why I was hurting, God did not bring me to Los Angeles to start my acting career and then leave me alone to become sick and die. He was right by me in the toughest of times and I know that He will continue to be with me in my future.

After becoming ill, getting this book out became even more important to me and not just for the purpose of saying I wrote a book. My desire is that you will read the poems that I have written and be able to connect to them in a way that will encourage and inspire you to continue on each and every day no matter the situation. I truly know that life is difficult and that everything may not seem like it's going your way but I am a witness that the trouble will not last forever. Every day is not promised and it is important that we remember this while we interact with our family, friends, co-workers and whoever else we might encounter on our daily journey.

The healing process for my body has just begun but I am proud to say that things are not like they were when I was at my lowest point. Recently I was told that I did not have Celiacs Disease, but was instead re-diagnosed with Ulcerative Colitis. This is a disease of the intestine that is also permanent. However, it is treatable and with the medicine that I have been prescribed, my health has gotten so much better. I have gained weight and strength back during this time as well and that in itself is a Blessing. I am also back on a regular diet of foods without having any side effects due to what I eat. Words cannot explain how thankful I am to be in this position after all that I went through. My future is bright and I look forward to many more years of acting, performing and writing.

The first poem that you will read is a poem that I wrote during the time of my sickness and trips to the Hospital. I felt that it would be a good way to start the book off with this poem and allow you to see the transformation that takes place from beginning to end. Again, I want to thank you for purchasing "Pen in My Hand". Enjoy…..

"KEEP ME IN YOUR PRAYERS"

The weight of my thoughts overpower me.
Blinded by my fears,
Believing my troubles will continue for eternity.
Turmoil and pain drain everything that I have.
Deaf ears to anything positive.
Fake smiles.
Silent laugh.
My future f-a-d-i-n-g away.
Closed eyes.
Tears falling.
And for some reason I still pray.
Asking God why?
I'm a good dude.
Not perfect,
But I try.
When will this end?
Whatever I did to deserve this I promise I won't do it again.

Some nights are hard to sleep.
I don't want people feelin sorry for me but this secret is too hard to keep,
Because it feels like I'm dyin….
And just the thought of those words "I'm dyin" tears me up inside
And next thing you know….I'm cryin.

This ain't me….

DAVID HUNTER JR.

I'm always the one who stays strong.
but at this moment I'm a fraction of half the man I was.
I feel bRokEn.

But it's just a feelin though.
Because things are turning around
Even if they are turnin slow.
And there's no time to waste complaining
Because I've got places where I want to go.
I've just been going through some things lately
And I needed to vent and let **somebody** *know.*

-Keep Me in Your Prayers

MY LIFE STORY

I'd like to share with you, a little bit of my life story. It all started back in 1985 in Northeast, Washington DC. Where this young man was born and came to be. I'll skip to my pre-school years; where I met my first boo. Her name was "Susie Q". She was 2. I missed about a week of school in 1st grade because of the flu. Didn't get to go on that field trip to the zoo. But, I never liked Animal Crackers anyway.

3rd grade had all the fine girls and that's where I learned how to become a man. This girl asked me to tie her shoe and I said I ain't tyin jack! Moms gave me a lil smack. Said I was actin way too bold. "But that smack ain't even hurt Mom. You getting kinda old".

Middle school and math were a problem. Numbers, factors, and equations, I just couldn't solve em. My teacher was Asian but spoke with a Caribbean accent, I was so confused. Eating dinner with my girlfriend from 11th grade not knowing which fork to use. 11 Spoons, 6 knives, and 3 forks?? I Love LA but ain't no city like New York. If you haven't been you should visit. Food is great. Nightlife exquisite. That place never stops movin. Kinda like me as a child. And that would explain why I was so wild. I could never settle down. At least, that's what my lady friend from sophomore year in college would say. She always said a lot. Seemed like it would never stop. Raining. That spring of 09'. I remember the rain because that's the day I met "MS. FINE." Asked her for her number and she replied, "why don't I give it to you the "next time"....you see me".

And man, that was rough. On my leg. When I fell off my bike and the kickstand went through my skin. Happened when I was 6. And I never rode a bike again. Fear crept inside my body and mind because the end was near. Only 2 more episodes of the Fresh Prince. Just thinking about that brought a tear, to my eye. Only question on my mind was why? Why were they so mean to the Bunny on the commercial for Trix?? They lied when they said words don't hurt as much as sticks…and stones.

Sometimes the peer pressure makes me want to give in and purchase one of these new phones. Just to be accepted. I played a lot of sports so in school I never was rejected. Projected, to be a pretty decent recruit. A few college coaches were in pursuit. But my grades were too low so they all thought I was slow and couldn't keep up with the fast pace of the big world I was in. Feeling alone in the Ocean of life with no raft and I couldn't swim. Only thing left to do was get on my knees and ask Him. For help. To keep me through life; Bring good fortune; A long career and a Beautiful wife. That knows how to cook, clean, sew, laugh, tell jokes, watch sports. And umm…not talk too much.

And there's nothing wrong with that at all. It would only enhance the relationship and make life great. Like Russell Crowe's acting in "A Beautiful Mind". Now that, that was an excellent movie. And I say "excellent" but my hippie friend says "groovy".

And that is what's so neat about people. We are all different and yet the same. Can scream and cheer with strangers that you don't even know their name. Just for the sake of a game. Or your favorite team. Now deep down inside I wish everyone was an Eagles fan, but hey, that's just my dream.

And honestly, that's probably silly. Cause not everybody can be from Philly. Or the inner city street. Where the intersections of "Harsh Reality" and "Bad Decisions" usually meet. I've seen a few of my friend's lives end before they could complete; their journey. Way too young to understand and comprehend the fact that life is so fragile and that you could be here today and gone today. The cliché'…is "here today/gone tomorrow". And for all of my lost friends I prayed to GOD that I could just borrow, a few more minutes and a few more days. Because HE said He'd give me everything if I'd just acknowledge Him in all my ways.

And I'm tryin. Not to get caught up in the little things. Just continuing to stay focused and continuing to bring, the same drive and desire each and every day. The determination and Joy that makes people wonder how I live this way. Well, honestly, it's not all me. So I don't deserve the credit and none of the Glory. But I am thankful for people like you. And I thank you for listening to everything that I've been through…so far…

A 3ʳᴅ GRADE LOVE

When I was in 3rd Grade. I used to color with a marker. The **BLACK** one. Cause deep down inside I always wanted to be a little bit darker. There was this girl in my class, whom I sat three rows behind. Playing "hide n go seek" and it was me who she'd always come find. Her name was Erica. The finest girl in school. We were reading buddies. All the boys thought I was cool. At this age going to school was something I really didn't mind. Recess, snacks, Erica and school ain't start till 9.

Thoughts of me and Erica going through my head. Teacher was teachin. Didn't hear a word she said. On the playground we played. I told her I liked her braid. On the hot days during recess, it was just us in the shade. I followed her and she followed me. Halfway through the year we carved our names in a tree. "Friends Forever" are the words we chose. I looked in her eyes. Then kissed her on the nose. I didn't know if I was allowed to kiss her. But then she grabbed my hand. She smiled and giggled. And I thought, well, I guess I can. I've met many girls, who I have memories of. But I'll never forget about my "3rd Grade Love".

"MOVIES ARE MY LIFE"

We started off as *Boyz N Da Hood*. Acting all wild trying to *Set It Off* each and every night. Doing the *Unthinkable* with no end in sight. The desire to build our own *Empire* constantly on our minds. Never once considering how *An Education* would help refine the young men that existed deep down inside of us.

Four Brothers going strong and there was no *Doubt* who you could trust. I could lean on them and they could *Lean On Me* too. *Bamboozled* into thinking we could do whatever we wanted to do. From our *Vantage Point* we were just some *Bad Boys* who only had an admiration for *Love and Basketball*. The heavy pursuit of *Brown Sugar* hunnies each and every *Friday*. Hoping and praying that the *Final Destination* would be inside a girl's bed after the *House Party*. Unaware that the *Raging Bull* inside of us was just normal teenage hormones.

Teachers always wanted to *Meet the Parents* to find out why we couldn't just *Do the Right Thing* in school. Threatening to split us up if our actions didn't change. But I wasn't really surprised. I *SAW* it coming *8 Mile* away. *Kicking and Screaming* about their decisions wouldn't work on this day. So I just decided to go along and change my ways. Considered a *Traitor* by my boys for many a days. And yet still I have no regrets.

Making that change in my life was like a personal *Independence Day*. No longer was I a *Man on Fire* believing there was always *A Time to Kill*. Instead I discovered I had *A Beautiful Mind* and used my *Gladiator* skills on the track and field. No longer was the message *Lost in Translation* from teacher to student. I was able to comprehend the *Higher Learning* I was receiving and able to gain knowledge and appreciate everything I was achieving. Made new friends. Started hanging with the *Goodfellas*. Met this pretty young girl and she became my heart. Just me and *My Fair Lady* hanging out. But things got *Rocky* and we ended up going our separate ways. I heard she lives in *Philadelphia* now. Must be nice. And even though she truly was an *American Beauty* I've moved on because *Boys Don't Cry* and I wasn't gonna start then.

Yet I'm still holding on to the memory of our early times together and thinking about that *Original Sin,* we committed. Felt bad about it for a little while but how can you resist the *Scent of a Woman*?

Honestly, sometimes it's just hard to say goodbye to yesterday and that *Cooley High* feeling you had when you were young and chillin during the *School Daze* with all your friends. But instead of focusing on the past I just continued to take it one day at a time. Reminding myself that others would have Loved to have been in my position. And everything happens for a reason. Just like the history of my people. They snatched us *Out of Africa* but now we living the *American Dream. Look Who's Talking now*!

I, MYSELF, AND ME

She is in Love. But I'm trying to help her see that right now, we can't be. Because I'm already in a relationship with I, Myself, and Me. At least that's the way it is in my mind. So I don't really have the time to waste. Even though her kiss is one of the sweetest things I could ever taste. I'm just focused on my career and the need to succeed suppresses all thoughts and images of her. She begs and pleads, telling me that I'm the one who can fulfill all of her needs. But the words just go in one ear and out the other. And yes, she's hurt now, but in a few years she'll recover. I hope…

Because these things always work out in the end. And being a bad husband is worse than being a bad friend. So I'm just trying to save her from all of the heartache and pain she would attain from attaching herself to this man right here. Some say I'm running away in fear because she is ready to marry. And the idea of one woman for the rest of my life is somewhat scary. But those claims I refute.

It's just that I've had this dream since I was a teen that one day I'd make it. And yes I do Love her but I'm not gonna fake it…and pretend. So I guess this is one battle that she's not gonna win. Such an abrupt end compared to how fast we started when we were about to begin…back then.

But that's life….

But I truly do believe she will make for a beautiful wife. Taking care of those 5 kids she wants to have; Providing for the family that she's always wanted. I'm pulling for her to have it all and hopefully one day she'll see everything the way that I saw. But I can't help but to be selfish at this point in my life. Giving all my time and energy to my family and my wife is not part of the plan right now. Things might be different one day. We'll just have to wait and see. Because I really do Love her. Just not as much as I Love me.

LONELY TEAR

You grabbed me by the hand.
Then you whispered in my ear.
You told me all your secrets
All your pain and all your fear.
You asked me if I Loved you
I pretended I didn't hear
You released my hand
Covered your face
Then cried a lonely tear.

SUBTRACTION

When I look at you, I see a perfect **10**. So many great things about you I don't even know where to begin. All this time I've been searching but you were right in front of my face. There's a lot of women in the world but none of them could take your place. Cause you're a **10**. But on second glance, I'm lookin and you not really THAT fine. Need a little more booty so Imma bump you down to a **9**. You still high on the list cause I Love women who stay on the grind and got a good head on their shoulders. Besides, Beauty ain't in the size of your butt; it's in the eye of the beholder. And yes, you are beautiful, even though your attitude ain't so great. Sometimes it feels like your brain is in its own little state. And that probably happens because you ain't no **9**. You're an **8**. Being a **9** is good but that was too much for your plate. Emotions running wild. Days filled with Love and days filled with hate. Sometimes you call me "baby" and then sometimes you get mad and threaten to call your brother Kevin. So yeah, I said **8**, but with emotions like yours you seem more like a **7**. Better get that hate out your heart or you won't make it into Heaven. I'm just being real. No games. No Tricks. Now you givin me that look which reminds me of a **6**. That's who you really are. Focused more on my clothes, my money and my car. But I'm not gonna complain. I just Thank God for being alive. And just having a girl is cool. Who cares if she's a **5**? A **5** means that you are ½ way good. And in a relationship you do ½ the things you should. Always quick to get a temper. And see right there I better just stop. Because all this fighting with you would just lead to me meeting a cop. Who will be bangin on my door. Asking me "what da problem is?" And my response is "she's a **4**!" And don't get upset. **4**'s are numbers people rarely forget....But if only I had a Crystal Ball. And could predict what life would be. I never would've guessed that I'd start with a **10** and end up with a **3**. That's the type of stuff that only happens on TV. And still, all I can think about is you. You look like a **3** but talk like a **2**. I'm all mixed up. Bout to go relax in the sun. And I want you there with me because after all I've said, I' still think you're the **1**!

THE DAY I FOUND LOVE

Our eyes connected.
And from that very moment
I knew my heart would no longer be neglected.
A guileless man with the bravado
To step to you correctly,
How could you reject it?

The beat of my heart racing.
At the thought of the pending rejection
I could be facing.
Only 33 seconds passed
Yet so many scenarios I thought of.
Proved to me inside, that you were the one,
And that's the day that I found Love.

"I WANT *ALL* OF YOU"

Tell me what it is that you desire. Tell me your most treasured secrets. Tell me the fears that cloud your mind. Tell me the memories of those hurtful nights buried so deep within that even God would have to search to find. Because I want ALL of you. I want the good and the great. I want the ugly and the bad. I want all of what you'll give me and all of what you never knew you had.

I want the curling of your lips when you smile. I want the captivating motion of your hips when you walk. I want the way that your eyes look at me every time that we sit and talk because you are incredible. The perfection of perfection. Worthy of my never-ending affection. A reflection of just how amazing God is.

I want the nights when you feel lonely. I want those times when you use no words but your eyes say hold me. I want the t-shirt and sweats days. I want the "I apologize for what I said earlier, I regret" days. I want the movie nights at the house and the Wednesday morning matiness. I want your dumb jokes. I want you singing your favorite song as loud as you can off note. Except, maybe for whenever I'm around.

I want your unique style and the classy way you dress. I want your loving and humble spirit and how you go out of your way just to Bless, others; who may not have as much. I want the soft and warmth caressing of your touch. I want the 100% truth that you'll only share with me. I want the tears flowing from your eyes as I'm down on bended knee asking you to marry me. I want the home cooked meals. I want your grace and your sex appeal. I want your past, your present and your future; never wanting to relinquish this feeling that only you can make me feel because I want ALL of you. I want the good and the great. I want the ugly and the bad. I want all of what you'll give me and all of what you never knew you had.

I want your attitude and the way you roll your eyes. I want your mind. I want your body. And I especially want the way that your thighs look right after you've just finished working out. I want the way you take control, your tremendous confidence and the impressive lack of doubt that exists within your frame.

I want your sick days. I want your am I getting fat or am I just kinda thick days. I want your aspirations and your goals to be achieved. I want your intellect and support. Believing in me when no one else would believe. I want your faith in God. I want your passion to do what's right. I want your Love to last forever and not just for one lustful night because I want ALL of you.

I want the good and the great. I want the ugly and the bad. I want all of what you'll give me and all of what you never knew you had.

……I want ALL of you……

A BLESSING WITHIN A BLESSING (4 MY MOTHER)

You have a strength deep inside
That even you cannot hide.
When I am down and feeling alone
It is in you who I confide
My guide when I am stressing
You're a Blessing within a Blessing
And I Love You!

FOR MY FATHER

Ever since my eyes could see
You're the man I've always wanted to be.
I thank you for your guidance.
I thank you for your love.
I thank you for your chastisement,
and your wisdom sent from above.
As men sometimes it's hard to speak
what's on our mind aloud.
But I do love you with all my heart
And I pray I make you proud.

DAVID HUNTER JR.

THE PATH I TAKE

With closed eyes, Alone I stand.

Looking into the mirror of life

trying to imagine who I am,

and where do I go from here?

It feels as if the end is near.

The walls of doubt surround my mind

as I try to find my way.

No light shines on the path I take.

The decision to follow my Dream now

feels like a mistake.

My confidence is low, and at any time, could break.

But deep down inside, a light shines bright.

My eyes open wide and I think I just might,

continue on this path towards my Dream.

With my eyes opened wide,

things are better than they seem.

TIRED, YET INSPIRED

Tired, yet inspired,

to continue on the path that God wants me to be on.

Distractions and temptation are around me every day but I know where my help comes from.

I have no choice but to make it.

"DEEPER AND DEEPER"

From time to time, thoughts, ideas and words form inside my mind and then I convert them into a rhyme. Sometimes the rhymes are funny and then sometimes they are serious and the message gets *"Deeper and Deeper"*.

Like back in the day when I was young. Seeing the pictures of slaves and reading up on the history that involved people who had dark skin like me. Black people hangin from a tree. 7 years old and I'm like "nah, this can't be". A change occurred instantly inside my brain. More knowledge I had to obtain because I needed an answer as to why they were treated this way. Told my Grandmother that slavery was wrong and sarcastically she responded, "Nah, ya don't say". But I was glad that I learned what I did. It helped me to discover secrets being hid. And other things that would have an impact on my life.

"Deeper and Deeper"…

The little girl always listens to Daddy when he tells her to come sit on his lap. She doesn't think anything's wrong when he whispers in her ear and says to her, "just play along". See, Daddy is sick in the head but baby girl don't know it. And she's affected by all the "love" from Daddy but she would never tell or show it. And now she's a hooker at the age of 19 who is addicted to sex and men who take advantage of her, because that's all she's ever known. But nobody really cares about hookers addicted to drugs anyway. You know why? Because they're hookers addicted to drugs so why waste your time?

PEN IN MY HAND

"Deeper and Deeper"

Like when Martin Luther King Jr. spoke of better days and had a hope that people would change their racist ways. But nowadays we've included straights vs. gays in this battle to prove what is right and what is not. It'll never stop. Even though the King had a Dream that one day we'd all be on the same team. Pressing towards a seemingly un-realistic future where Love and respect would exist. A life often referred to as Heaven on Earth would be bliss. But Dr. King would be amazed at how all the Love he spoke of was just a phase that came and went. Tempers have since flared and anger has conquered almost every soul. Over 40 years since his speech about a Dream and still so far from his goal. Fighting inside our community is resolved quickly with just a trigger… from the gun of our mouths as we continue to call each other Nigger. Tearing down instead of building up. Not even thinking of our future but just focused on today. People dying young because you cannot live *this* way. We're running out of graves as we continue to dig ourselves…

"Deeper and Deeper"…

You can't reach for your future while hanging on to your past. And why try to hang on to something that wasn't meant to last? Because if it was meant to be it would be. We are living in the day and age of "Hey everybody!! Look at me!" Selfishly selfish when it comes to everything that we do. And even if this poem lived to be 500 years old it could never be more true. The object of life is not just to maintain and sustain. And it's not about finishing first or gaining as much as you can gain. It's about having the ability to share the Love to our young brothers and sisters so that we can help ease the pain…of their hearts. But with a lack of leadership in our community where do we start? That's the question of the hour as we continue to search for the power that will help us succeed and reach the full potential of where we should have been. A long, long, time ago.

WITHOUT LOVE

As I write, I'm looking at the clock and it's 11:46 at night. I can't sleep. Already said my prayers and asked the Lord my soul to keep. Till the next day. My heart beating fast. Why do I feel this way? It's all because of you. I've tried to ignore it before but now I know it's true. You're constantly on my mind. In almost every thought. All my life I've been runnin from Love but now I'm tryna get caught. I even tried buyin Love before but then I realized Love can't be bought…or sold. And that's what I was told. When I was young. But I was dumb. Just lookin for the girl who was fast and would give me some. But then I got a lil older. And the nights have gotten colder. And I'm sittin at home, alone, wishin that I would have told HER, everything. How much I Loved her voice and the way she could sing. How beautiful she was and how much she meant to me. Instead I was stupid, never thinking what life would be… Without Love.

NOT A CLOUD IN THE SKY

Not a cloud in the sky
But I'm seein the rain.
Not a scratch on my body
But I'm feelin the pain.

Got so much to say
Don't know which words to use.
But to let you just leave.
Now that... I refuse.

Why did this happen?
When did it begin?
When did I become just..."another person"
And not..."More than a friend"?

Something just ain't right
And I really don't know
Your mouth says "it's cool"
But your eyes are saying "just go!"

Well that's what Imma do
Imma let you go be
Let you go make up your mind
Let you go be free.

I really don't want to
But I also want what's best for us.
And I'd rather be single, happy and your friend.
Then be together, hurt, and always fuss.

DAVID HUNTER JR.

I'll still be thinking of you
Like almost all the time
I hope you get whatever you're looking for
And someday I'll find mine...

FRIEND

You been there since the beginning
You said you wouldn't leave until the end.
You were there for me, when it wasn't "cool"...
When it wasn't "cool" to be my friend.

Through the ups and downs. The highs and lows.
You never left my side
When all else failed and no one else was around.
You consoled me as I cried.

We laughed
We joked
We fought
We argued

But after everything
You always stayed.

You're the friend I always wanted.
....And I'm glad we met...

YESTERDAY

YESTERDAY was a bad day. YESTERDAY, I lost my best friend. I don't know why GOD took him. But I know one day I'll see him again. I know this for a fact. Because we made a pact….that we would be there for one another…until the end.

My friend was a great dude. He was what people should be about. No matter what the situation would be, you never heard a bad word outta his mouth. YESTERDAY was a bad day. And I still can't believe it's true. People ask me will I be alright? And real talk, I don't know what Imma do.

I remember the good days. Those dances at school. When all you needed was a fresh cut and some sneakers. All the girls thought you was cool. We used to walk around the street. Not a thought on our brain. Because every day was different, yet everyday was the same. Just happy being around each other. My mom was like his mother. And don't yall laugh but yall remember them sleepovers under the same cover.

It's kinda hard for me. To tell you how I feel. I can't even explain it. It's all so surreal.

YESTERDAY was a bad day. YESTERDAY I lost my best friend. And even though YESTERAY was 10 yrs ago…I still miss him!!

IRREPLACEABLE

The world is a funny place
And they say there are a lot of things that you can't replace.
I never thought any of this to be true.
That is until, I met you…

BEFORE YOU EMBRACE TOMORROW

Before you embrace tomorrow
You have to let go of yesterday
You have to first forgive yourself
Then humble yourself and pray.

Take some time alone
Spend it with the Lord
Protect your mind and your soul
With the Bible as your sword.

God knows your heart.
And His desire for you is to have only the best.
He'll bring you into your future
Allowing you to see that yesterday was only a test.

THOUGHTS

There's a battle of control in my mind.
But the controls up there,
are all set to re-wind.
Taking me back to a place where I've been.
Thoughts telling me that "you'll never be as good as them".
Thoughts of doubt.
Thoughts of confusion.
I begin to think these thoughts aren't real.
But that thought fades away like an illusion.
There's been an intrusion.

Who is here?

Why are you clouding my mind with fear?
The silence continues to gROW.
So many thoughts in my mind,
Yet so much I don't know.
At the crossroads of life
Un-aware of the direction I should go…

MY VICE

I've broken up with you so many times before times twice. But as you already know I keep coming back because you're my vice. My guilty, yet temporary fulfilling pleasure. So clever and so comforting are our times together so I'm unable to notice the effect you're having on my life.

You see, my mind is conflicted; making me believe that I'm being restricted if I don't give in. 101 out of 100 times you always win; and I lose…

(And I hate losing)

So if I give in I am thus now choosing to win. But in the end I find myself back in the familiar place of when did "this" begin? "This", being my negligence or selective Amnesia when I hear your voice whispering "I just wanna please ya"…My Vice.

Why don't you ever play nice? I've broken up with you so many times before times twice and yet still, here you are. I run away from you knowing you're not good for me but I never stray too far.

Because deep down I'm scared of the unknown. You've been with me for so long and now that I'm grown it's difficult to let you go. Even if inside of my heart I truly do know that you and I must head our separate ways. And it may hurt to hear me say this but I can't look back at you or gaze because then I just might stay. Our relationship has been nothing but a game of Tug of War and I'm getting too old to play.

And these words may seem harsh or mean. But you make me feel dirty and I just want to be clean.

I know you don't believe me and you say we'll meet again. But your involvement in my life is over and I am removing your title of "friend". There's no more room in my life for you. Where you once lived someone else now stays. And for the rest of my nights and for the rest of my days, I'll never forget this moment; the moment that you and I parted ways…

TUG OF WAR

The struggle in my mind is like a tug of war. The Evil sounds so good but I'm tryna ignore. They say life's a game but I hope they not keeping score. Cause I feel defeated. Feels like someone cheated because I can't win. Every time I think I'm good, here comes the sin. One side of my brain is like "Who let him in?" But the other side of my brain is like "let the fun begin!!" I pray, and ask for a change. Father, please forgive. Yes I did wrong but I just cannot live, without you in my life. I won't even dare try. The Struggle is so intense sometimes I just cry. And when I cry, I shake. Too much pain on my mind, don't know how much more I can take. Why me Lord? Why can't I change? I know you see my heart is true. And there's nothing else that I'd rather do, than be made whole. The struggle in my mind is a distraction keeping me from trying to achieve my goal. Evil trying to take my mind so that it can also have my soul. My mind is flooded with thoughts I didn't think were possible for me to conceive. Evil thoughts taking over, or at least that's what they try and make me believe. But I refuse to let this trouble be. Corrupt and Doubtful thoughts cannot reside in me. It's just a Tug of War inside my mind. And even though I'm constantly being pulled, I've made up my mind that Evil no longer has me fooled...

…..The Game is Over…..

"IF I COULD JUST BELIEVE"

He told me that there would be many Blessings for me to receive, if I could just Believe. And that in my lifetime, if I trusted in Him, many accomplishments I would achieve. But what a shame it is, when my Faith in God is not as strong as His, Love was for me. My eyes were open but I was refusing to see; what He had in store. Instead of thanking Him for what I had, I'd only ask for more. Continuously failing the tests of life because I did not prepare. Did not read my Bible. Wasn't even thinking about prayer. Then had the nerve to speak the words "Life isn't fair."

See in my time of living, you could never question my giving, or my attendance to the many different services throughout the week. Proclaiming that No One Else could receive the Glory. Quick to grab the mic and tell the testimony of my life story. Inside the walls of the church my belief in God was oh so strong. I was a preacher's kid. I played the Drums. And knew almost every song.

But after the Benediction; I lost all my Conviction, for doing sin. And playing with God is a game that you will never win. But, I tried. Got in trouble for my sins. Told God I'd never do it again. But, I lied. Kept on playing until I almost lost everything. And then, I cried.

It seemed like all hope had disappeared. No longer trusting in the Lord. I was living my life in fear. I even remember crying after I told God about all the changes I wanted to make for the New Year; because I felt alone. All these years of private tears because something inside was not right. God was calling me and I was tired of trying to fight, against his plan.

He had to bring me down to my knees before I could truly understand, that faith is the substance of things hoped for and the evidence of things not seen. 28 years old and now I fully comprehend what that means. And I'm so thankful. That I've been givin the time to correct my mistakes or at least not make them again. Believing and knowing in my heart that Jesus is more than just my Savior. He's my best friend. And no matter how bad my behavior was He shed His Blood to cover the sin.

And I would be remiss, if I lived my life never acknowledging a Love as great as this. More than a Love between Husband and Wife. More than a passionate kiss. He died for me. Gave up His soul. Had His body ripped apart just so mine could be made whole. And I'm a Believer. No longer just a "Sunday Morning Christian". No longer an under achiever. I'm just good. Striving to be the man that God always knew I would…become.

No longer worried about the battle because it's already been won. And I am oh so thankful that my Father sent His son….for me…

THE AGAPE WAY

In the midst of my life and through all the struggles and trials, I just think about how good God has been to me and how I am able to still smile, because I'm His child. He's Loved me from my first breath and even though sometimes I've felt alone, I realize that He's never left.

God can't help but to Love us. Even when we falter and aren't worthy of His trust. God's Love is everlasting. And the best way to experience His Love is through Faith, Prayer, and Fasting. It might seem like a lot to do but it really doesn't take much. You don't have to get all extra Traditional to receive God's un-conditional Love. All He asks is that you accept Him into your life and acknowledge that He sent His Son from up above. Treat others as you would like to be treated. Displaying nothing but Love upon your countenance because you are not defeated. Even in the times of the storm, God's Love is able to protect and keep you warm.

No other Love can even come close. Not even the back in the day, track #2 on a CD playing some Marvin Gaye on constant replay will make you feel this kinda way.

...It's called, AGAPE LOVE...

A Love from God to His people. Men and Women all created equal. Each one of us original in our own right. Created with the Love of God inside of us so there's no reason we should have to fight, amongst each other. Whether connected by blood or not, you're my brother and I Love ya. The Agape Way is truly the only way to be. Regardless of if you're from Sacramento or Washington D.C. I just pray that we, can get back to the way it was. When you didn't need a reason to show Love to someone, you did it just because.

So it is a must, that we continue to believe in our Lord and Savior. The Creator of life and the judge of our behavior. The One who desires for us to Love our neighbor, more than we Love our own lives. And Blessings will flow down upon those that genuinely try, and keep this commandment. However hard it may be and even if you don't understand it. There is no greater Love.

And that is the reason why I continue to smile. Even in the midst of my struggles and through each and every trial. His Love lets me know and feel that I am still His child. And that everything I've been through will be all worth the while because Love is the greatest gift you can give. So I promise to Love the Agape way for the rest of the days that I live.

DREAM AND A PRAYER

I don't have much
Besides a Dream and a Prayer
That in the future
Exists a Love that both you and
I will share
A Dream that our Love
Will last for eternity
No thoughts about anything besides
You and Me
Continuously
Becoming one
Under the sun
And the moon
And if we parted ways before
Forever
It would be too soon.

DAVID HUNTER JR.

FROM HER EYES TO MINE

*All it took was a glance
To make me take that chance.
From her eyes to mine,
It seemed like the two of us meeting each other
had been pre-designed.
A sexy complexion.
Body ready for affection.
In need of a man in her life
To provide both pleasure and protection.
I was
A rookie to this feeling,
In need of direction.*

*Life passing by
With every second wasted.
I'm so close to my heart's desire
I can almost taste it.
They say Real Love doesn't exist
And that's not true.
It just may be that it
hasn't happened yet for you.*

*But, for me, on this day,
A young man,
With no words to say,*
Love, at first sight, occurred.
*And because I took that chance,
Life has never been better.*

JUST THE SAME

Deep inside the memory banks of my mind, pictures and thoughts of her is what you would find if you really wanted to take your time, to locate the evidence that you seek.

You and I were an item, but thoughts of her and I being together had me dreaming of better days. She had me experiencing these falling in love even though I just met her days. And it was only one night but I just couldn't forget her days. Optimistic and prayerful that those feelings weren't just a phase.

The truth of the matter is that I never once physically cheated. But every impure thought of her was happily greeted and mis-treated; thus turning from admiration into a bad habit that could not be defeated because all I did was feed it, until it grew out of hand.

And I'm sharing this with you hoping that somehow you might understand that I truly meant no harm.

But as I look into your eyes, at this very moment I now realize, that the result of my actions has severely damaged what we had; causing you tremendous hurt and pain. And although I never once physically cheated; wandering eyes along with an imaginative mind makes it all feel just the same.

DREAMS OF JUNE

All through the night, I Dream of June. The anticipation builds and my excitement grows but I need not speak too soon. Closed eyes with an open heart. Ready to embark on a journey into the unknown. What will happen? That is the question that continues to run through my head. I prepare my words while I Dream so that when I wake I'll remember what I said. Because THIS time, has to be perfect…

SO many words I'd like to use. Searching for the right ones to choose. I want to find the answers to my problems that for many years have gone un-solved. Holding on to hope that this time will be different. When he left, he said he'd be back in June. I haven't seen him since the age of 5. Trying to figure out where he went? What he's doing? And if he's still alive? I believe he will return one day. So I continue to Dream of June. But the years have passed, he has yet to return and I don't understand why. My Dreams of June are crushed, with the reality of life, that May will always skip to July.

"LIKE FATHER-LIKE SON"

See, I'm out here trippin, runnin around in this world. Thinking I'm ready to settle down, and I say that to every girl. I be like wow, look at your eyes, look at your lips, look at your waist. And before you say one word let me tell you that I ain't afraid to taste.

See I know I be lyin, but I really be tryin…to come at you correct, cause believe me I respect every single thing my father taught me. But that's a lie….cause he wasn't there…I don't know why, nigga was prolly scared. That's ok though. I ain't need him anyway.

Back to you…and back to all the things I wanna do…ooops, my bad. Did that offend you? Let me rub your head, whisper in your ear. Tell you all these things that'll make your eyes tear.

Say things like "I'll never leave you". And "baby, imma be there till the end". And as soon as I got you…I'm out. I'm just a man. Cant' you understand? Your name is "wo-MAN" so you part of me. So dat means you gots to see how I truly be. I can't help it. That's just how I do. I don't believe myself when I say I don't need help. I know I do.

I love you with all my heart and I wanna be with you forever. And as we begin to hug I glance behind you and see that girl in the light grey sweater that fits her chest OH so right!! If only I could have her, just for one night. And see, that's where my fun begins. The beginning… of the end. Yeah I may have lost you but I'm sure you'll make it. You're a tough chick. That's why I love you. You can take it. Just pray for me tho. Cause I really need the Lord and I need help.

And without you, this feelin I would have never felt. It's crazy cuz I'm crazy. I can't get you off my mind. And I'm quick as ever to make up an excuse or lie my way out. But never just be real with you. Now what's that all about?

I have this idea, of what a man should be.
And nowhere in that idea do I see a picture of me.

I take a lot of the blame. Cause a lot of my faults were mine. So many events which took place that changed my outlook. Things that rocked my world and had me shook. I was out there scared. Part of me still is.

Why couldn't my dad just take care of what was his?
He left me hangin….
And that's why I gotta leave you.
Because in all honesty…
That's the 1 thing….he taught me how to do…

MR. MIS-UNDERSTOOD

When you've done something wrong for so long, how do you call it quits? Depriving yourself of the need to get a hit could cause a mental fit. Some type of distress in your mind. An un-expected chemical in-balance in your body is what you will find, if you end it right here. And it's clear, the time to stop is now. Only thing preventing the change is the question in your mind of HOW?

How do I make this right? Secretly hoping that a miracle can occur overnight and finally, the pain comes to an end. Emotions still in shambles because it feels like you're about to lose a best friend. Who was there for you time and time again.

A helpful snort that left you with this constant sniff. Maybe it was the whole bottle or maybe just a 5th. But you're not addicted. Been arrested for illegal substances before but you weren't convicted. So you're fine. You're just Mis-understood.

Been lookin for a job and you really is tryin. Went searchin all day and everybody say "we ain't hirin". Went home, told your wife and she said "somehow I know you lyin!". Those hurtful words pushed you to drugs and you living your life but close to dyin...in your mind. How do I make this right? This question constantly on the tip of your tongue. And yes it's quite difficult to stop something you started when you were so young. Because it feels so good. Sometimes you think stopping is what you probably should...do. But that thought alone simply blows your high. And stopping is just another word for quitter and you're not that guy. So let's just continue and give this thing one... more... try. And then everything will be alright...

How did it get to be like this? Was it the absence of your father? The lack of a Mother's hug and kiss? The answer is no because to you they never did exist. Who are You? What is your name? Mr. Mis-understood? Ohhhh, I see. That's who you be. A junky in denial. Now that would make for good reality TV.

Placing the blame upon others. Hoping that nobody cares enough about you to come snatch off the covers, of your lies. You've got children growing up with hate in their hearts praying the words "I hope my daddy dies". And you don't even care. Because they don't really know how it feels inside. An intense addiction to the drug infliction is something you're trying to hide, because of pride. Not willing to let go. Even if in your heart you really do know, that by continuing on this path, the end is near. But there's no fear. Everything is all good. You're not really a bad person, just Mis-understood.

POETIC POLITICS

This poem is not Political. So all my Poet friends and people that are critical, take out your pen. And number from 1 to one-hundred and ten. Cause I'm bout to begin. I'm sorry, but I'm not gonna talk about the troops in Iraq and about how 60% of our soldiers go overseas and only a third come back. I'll just be wastin time talking about D.C. crime or the gangs in Chicago and MS-13. I'd rather talk about that new song and dance and how it reminds me of the "shoulder lean", that we used to do back in the day. When e'rybody was in the closet but now e'rybody....

Half the country sayin "Yes We Can". Half the country sayin "no you won't: Half the country replies "I bet we will". Half the country says "I bet you don't". Because of the Hurricane, New Orleans and parts of Mississippi still need help. But instead of giving the money to them we paying $5 million for a new telescope so that we can see Orion's belt. More clear...

All the way up there in the sky. WHY?? Don't ask me. Ask the person or people in charge of all this reality TV. Nonsense if you ask me. Over 20,000 homeless in "the city of Angels" but from the outside in it all looks so pretty. This world's got issues but all you'll hear is an excuse about the abuse that takes place day out and night in. According to the Bible, half the stuff we doin now is called a Sin. But that's just if you ask Him. The Man upstairs. Yeah you know Him. The one you talk to at night when you say your prayers. Maybe you don't understand what I'm sayin and you're just un-aware. I'm not just sayin this cause I care. I'm just letting it out because all this was inside and my thoughts flow into words and my words you ride...like a wave.

And please behave. Little Black boy in class. One more peep outta you and that's your Black ass! And back to the Ghetto you go....

...Hey, did you know, that HIV is one of the top killers of African American Women and Men? I didn't think you did. But now you do. Maybe now you'll think different when someone asks you to donate funds or time. And some of yall thinking, "Now that was a weird line. The word "do doesn't go with "time". But see this ain't just some rhyme. There's a message in the speech. And a different way I like to teach. No discrimination. Everyone I'm tryna reach. And I know this ain't church. Just chill. I ain't tryna preach. I just need your attention. Gotta keep you locked in like Mike Leach.

When it comes to poetry, I'm an Oscar winner like *Kramer vs. Kramer*. Take a picture of my poem. Buy a frame. It's a framer. In life, things happen unexpectedly. Like people from high school sending me friend requests on Facebook when back in the day they never accepted me... But this poem is not Political so don't yall get all critical when I don't talk about poverty. Or all the people who are in need. All those kids in the commercial who with 39 cents a day you could feed. Instead, I'll just turn my swag on. When I hop up outta bed. Meanwhile, another car bomb has gone off. 37 DEAD.

The interior design in my mind is refined. I'm in the zone. And I ain't really into all these new phones so don't expect me to be impressed by your new $847 cell. Some don't like what I'm sayin but I hope it rings a bell. Life ain't nothing but show and tell.

And it's time to do an about face. If you had no food to eat everyday how would that taste? Trade your car in for a bike. You'd think it was a joke waiting on somebody to yell "sike", or prank. So many Blessings we receive and we don't thank. We just run...our mouth. Sayin all types of stuff. Like "man, only $500 in my account. Man, my life is rough".

I told yall this poem is not Political. It's only the Truth. We need more women like Ruth. Not Lil Kim. Confusin our kids so that when they see people they say "was that a her or a him". It's all a big mess. But

I'm ready to clean. Raise your hands high if you understand what I mean.

Now all this talking done got me spent. Opened my mouth for 2 seconds and look where the time went. I wasn't tryna vent But I did. No more trips to the airport to watch the planes land like when I was a kid. Be careful, or they will arrest you. And I know some of them must wanna test you. But it's nothing new. And why is the White House more of a zoo than the zoo?

But I ain't tryna get all Political. So please put down your pens. I'm done being critical. The world will just go on bein pitiful. Cause that's the way it goes. Full of selfish people all logged on to ME.COM and it shows.

But a change gon come soon. At least I think it might. And until that change comes we must continue to keep up the fight.

HER, HIM AND THEM

She's got that fire that has all the boys trying to inquire, all the information they can, about who she is, and if she's his; or, if she's able to just hang out and chill. Listening to all their lies as they go in for the kill, trying to steal, what GOD gave to her. She doesn't know it, but she's got the power to say no. Nothing wrong with wanting to take it slow. First becoming friends, and, even if it doesn't work out yall can still be cool when it ends, and, maybe sort of try and mend your differences together. But it's hard for her because she developed quick and got all the guys trippin over their d**k. Fighting to get her approval. They finally wear her down and begin to deflower her flower. Got her trippin and sendin "I Love You" texts every single hour but she receives no reply. Heart broken and depressed, giving in to the notion that all guys lie. Another dude wanna talk to her but they warn him "I wouldn't even try, because she's all messed up". And it really wasn't her fault. She was just another victim to the system, of trying to fit in.

He's sittin at home all alone. Eatin lunch, watchin TV when he hears the ring of his phone. And, it's her. His voice drops about 8 octaves into this deep ass purr. And the game begins to flow outta his mouth. He's a smooth talker with a little twang in his speech because he's from the South. He's not in Love with her but he says it a lot. She gives him head when he says it so even though he doesn't mean it, he just can't stop. He knows that besides the sex the relationship really doesn't mesh. But he's too stubborn and not willing to shut off his flesh, and step away. Because if he turns down some sex all the fellas will think that he's gay. So he continues to do what he does. Doin it just because. Knocking on the door to trouble, because sexing her down without a condom is like asking for a double…shot…of stupid. Mixed with a little bit of "what were you thinking?" But he can't stop now cause he's a drunk and he just keeps on drinking, his way down into a mess. 14yrs old with a kid. Not because he Loved her, but because sex in the 9th grade is what everybody else did. And at least now they know…that he ain't gay. Just another victim to the system of trying to fit in.

They were at this party. Music loud, blastin in their ears. Laughin and havin fun. On their 6th and 7th beers. Never had a drink before but I guess now's the time to start. You see, they couldn't get into the party without taking a shot. 3hrs into the party and everybody's name they done forgot. They got in and that's all that really mattered. Now they are cool and everyone tells them how much fun they are when they're wasted. 4 o'clock the next morning, the word spreads around. "Did you hear about them, and what the police found?" A totaled car, laid on its back, smashed into a pole. They both had dreams. Hard to believe this was their goal. But man, what a night. Way to live it up and have fun. Even though they never made it to the next day to see the next sun, rise up and shine bright. They sure did have a hell of a night. They just wanted to party. And party they did. And even though they died, their story is not much different from Him, with the kid. And don't forget about Her. And all of her messed up memories of people in the past. All of these individuals victims of trying to grow up too fast.

We all know a "Her", "Him", and a "Them". These are just some of the stories in the everyday lives for young women and men and it's gotta change. Because we don't need any more victims to the system, of trying to fit in.

SPECIAL BOND

Lookin into my daughter's eyes. Every day for her, I want to be a surprise. I tell her she's my heart and watch her face glow. I let her know this every day. My emotions never sway as long as she's ok. I told her I Loved her. She just stared back and then simply said, "Daddy, why do you snore?" I wanted an "I Love you too Daddy" but her honesty was something I could not ignore. A face like hers you can only adore. And besides, you can't get mad. She's only 4

There are some times when she doesn't think I'm so great. Like those times when I say turn off the TV., it's getting late. She's got a cookie in one hand, and she ask for another. She gives me this look that reminds me of her mother. Then here she goes, "But Daddy please, I finished everything on my plate. And even though it wasn't good I ate everything I didn't wanna ate". But I don't give in. And she gets mad. Stomps up the stairs mumbling "I wish you weren't my dad". I know she doesn't mean it. I realize she's just upset. But words like "I wish you weren't my dad" are words that I'll never forget.

As she gets older, gone are the days of her crying on my shoulder. She's out in the world. Living her life. I just pray she remembers everything that I told her. She's a young woman now, full of Beauty and Pride. Exuding confidence with every step in her stride. Our time together has dwindled down. Nowadays I'm not the only man in town. She's met this boy. Another guy in her life. Who sees her for the great woman she is and one day, might ask her to be his wife. Being that my daughter is only 16 I'm not in a rush for that to come true…

But she is dating. Something that does not thrill me. Just the thought of a boy touching her. I think that thought is trying to kill me. Which is why I don't think about it. "Just be in by 10 and please….please don't go on a date again!" That's my thought. I just pray it instead of say it. Keeps the mood light. And prevents the usual father-teenage daughter fight. Never been a dad before but I sure hope I'm doing it right.

The College years. Some of my biggest fears. Dropped her off at school. Drove home alone. Some of my biggest tears. Every time the phone rang I just prayed it wasn't something I didn't wanna hear. She was out of my control. There was no one there to stop her from going out or drinking this or smoking that…I raised her the only way I knew how, but was it enough?

4 years of college complete. No job. No money, so to dad she will retreat. Just for a while. Until she's back on her feet. Can pay her own bills, buy nice clothes and afford to eat. Even now, while she's home, it's just not the same. All grown but even more now. I can't put my finger on it but something has changed. I ask her "what's good?...you alright?" She replies "I'm fine", but I know that line "I'm fine" really means "no, I'm not OK but I'll say it anyway just to make you go away and stop bothering me"…I know what to do…I think. Honestly, no I don't. I'm lost. I need help…Maybe I should get the belt? Nah, what am I talking about? She's a grown woman. Let her be…

Being a parent is so complex

These days, It's like a hit or miss. I know something is wrong when not even a father's kiss can rectify my daughter's pain. I'd like to say I've done everything I can but as a man. I can't understand that things do not happen like you plan or want them to.

Came home from work. It was late one night. Before I went to sleep. I had to say goodnight. Started to say my prayers as I walked up the stairs to her room. Opened the door. Tears filled my eyes. She wasn't there…

But there was a note. That my daughter wrote. She left it on her bed. In it were words. But not too many. Here is what it said:

> *"I Love you daddy. It's not your fault. I'm sorry you had to find out like this. But , I just couldn't take it anymore. Life is too much for me right now and I'm only 24. I know it's only going to get worse. You have done an amazing job and I'm grateful to have had you for a father. You showed me what a real man is. Unfortunately, there's nobody out here even close to you. It's depressing and I'd rather die than live single my whole life in the care of my father. Well, that's all. Just remember that I'll always be your little girl. Good Bye…"*

As you might've guessed, my daughter is gone now. She committed suicide. I wish I could've done something to keep her alive. Grab her by the hand. Help her understand that she's only 24. She's young. She'll get a man. But it's too late. I wonder if this would have happened if she weren't overweight?

You see, my daughter was a big girl. That's why she needed so much Love. Being made fun of. Taking your father as your prom date. I knew these weren't ideal circumstances but I didn't think they'd take her from me. A depressed, overweight young woman. Who truly was a Joy To The World. A one of a kind, kind've girl. But this is where my story ends. Only thing left of my daughter is a memory and a few friends. Who visit every now and then. Thank GOD for them.

"To My Daughter"
I don't know where to begin
More than a daughter, you were my friend
So sad your time here had to end
I need you…

PEN IN MY HAND

I Love you. And miss you.
Just to hold you. And kiss you
Is all I want.

You're smile, the laugh you had.
That special way that you said "dad"
I'm so thankful and so glad
I knew you…

GOD PLEASE BLESS

God Please Bless. Just 3 simple words I say to help ease the stress, that invades my life every now and then. God tells me that He's going to assist me in my time of trouble just like He's done again and again. But, when things don't get changed at exactly the point or time I want, or need them to, sometimes I ask the question Why? Why won't He help me? Is He even listening to me? God made the sun, moon, and the Earth so I'm pretty sure that He can see; that I need some help. Because in this world that we live; it really doesn't take much for us to give, up, or give in, to the temptation and frustration of trying not to sin. Staying consistent in our walk with God so that we don't slowly blend in with everyone else around us. But He's not responding to my prayers so in God do I really trust?

God Please Bless. Just 3 simple words I say to help ease the stress. Please help me to get out of this financial mess. I've got two bank accounts and $3 combined. It's been two weeks since I've sinned and I even repented this time. And please, don't mistake my requests for complaints. I just need your help so that I'll be able to show some restraint when I experience these attacks on my mind, body and soul. To be more like you, a Blessing to others and reach Heaven is my goal. But for right now…What do I do about this sin? These lustful thoughts and urges that occasionally arise from within. Reminiscing about yesterday's transgressions and those fleshly desires I pursued. God Please Bless me with the remembrance that I am a child of Yours and my life has been re-newed.

God Please Bless. Just 3 simple words I say to help ease the stress. God is ready for me and I say I'm ready for Him to move on my behalf. But when I can't even quote a simple scripture to encourage someone else I'm sure He can't help but to be mad. And God, I really am trying to please you each and every day. Even though I mumble a prayer into my pillow as I roll out of bed each day, You understand what I'm tryna say…right?

I didn't think you did. And why would you respond to a person over the age of 21 who still prays like a little kid? So as of this moment, I'm askin. I'm prayin. And believing with all my heart that you'll be open to what I'm sayin. I'm sorry for my selfish prayers and my actions that were not pleasing to you. Forgive me for my sins and guide me on this Godly walk in everything that I do. Your son is the Savior. And this I confess. I am a changed person who still needs your assistance so God Please Bless!

NONCHALANT

Living in LA.
Chillin in DC
Everywhere and anywhere
Is where I wanna be
Can't worry bout yall
Too busy thinking bout me
≠I'm selfish

My girl wanna chill
I'm ready to go
Now we get to arguing
And someone hits tha flo
You hear somebody yellin
"Yeah, Yeah, you want some mo!?"
≠Call the police

A lot of people are weird
Some more than others
Broke up with my girl
She wouldn't share the covers
Kicked me out the house
I'm back living with my mother
≠I hate washing dishes.

Brought me a convertible
Decided to drop the top.
Drivin in my convertible
Saw a red sign that said stop
I just kept it movin

And that's when I saw the cop
≠I need a lawyer.

In my house getting dressed
Gotta interview at 1
I don't have a job now
But my next job will be fun
I wonder if mall security guards all get they own gun
≠I'm bout to get paid!

It's rainin outside
Can't go for my morning walk
Didn't pay my bill
Gotta cell phone, can't talk
Ran outta lotion
Ankles white as chalk
≠I got dandruff

38 and single
I think I need a girl
She said she want a man
I said I'd give her the world
She don't like me no more
Cause I ran over them little squirrels
≠I hate PETA

Asked could I stay the night
needed a place to rest my head
it's 2 AM. I'm WIDE awake
I think I wet the bed.
Hope she don't roll over

If she do I'm gon be dead.
≠I'm thirsty

Only 1 gift for Christmas
Moms got me a pet
A cat with 3 legs
I took it back to the vet
Doc was like, what can I do??
I said, what else can I get?
≠*worst gift* EVER!

PEN IN MY HAND

I ain't like most poets. And from that very first sentence I just said, you oughtta know it. Got a lot on my mind but don't show it. Dad said *"never lettem see you sweat"*. And I won't. I just keep writin. My life is exciting.

Like a taxi driver in New York, I'm always on the street. They gotta car. I use my feet. Walkin to and fro, never knowin who I'll meet. Music blarin through the air and I'm rockin to the beat. But I'm so discrete, when I'm spittin game. Got you telling me all your biz. And you don't even know my name! What a shame. These otha cats is lame. Exchangin favors and sellin out for fame.

It's a rush to the top. People want stuff fast. But not I. Never been that type of guy. I'm just observant and take note of what I see. And if I acted like you, then I wouldn't be me. But I gotta stay in the gym. Can't stop now or I'll look like him.

Mr. tobacco spittin. Mr. Ketchup and Mustard off the lip drippin. Mr. "Man, it's too tough. Man, I'm quittin."

See, some people mistake me for bein weak. Cause sometimes my words are jumbled when I speak. I tell them the idea was just in my head but then they like, "well that's not what you just said". So I try to relax my nerves. Count to ten. Take a deep breath. Then write my words with a pen.

I just jot down what I have to say. Cause sayin what I say can't be said any other way.

See I'm not like most poets. And I'm sure by now you know it. Not a poet with technique. But a poet that's unique. Got the ladies smiling cause I'm smart with a physique. They say "oooh, he kinda fine. No kids. Single AND he's educated??...Get out tha way girl! He mine!"

But before they even begin. I tell them that nothing comes between me and this pen. See these ladies like me now. But this pen has been there from the start. These ladies speak to me off the visual. But this pen speaks from the heart.

And no matter how fine you are. Nothin will ever tear us apart.

There's just something about this pen. It's like having the perfect best friend. Been there from the beginning. Won't leave until the end.

See I'm not like most poets. And I'm sure by now you know it. A lot of people TELL you what they're about. But me, I'd rather show it.

I'm just a man with a pen. And a desire since I was 10. That when I got older, my words people would comprehend.

Like Dr. King, I had a dream. That most people didn't understand. But now things are different.

All because of this pen in my hand.

IMMA POET AND I KNOW IT

Imma poet and I know it.

Been Blessed with the gift to formulate rhymes with my words and I won't throw it, away. No matter what distractions come in my life and despite what the critics might say. Because I was born to write. The messages of encouragement and the ability to enlight, those who choose to listen.

You see, we all have a story or two that exists deep inside. The only difference between you and I is my willingness to share and confide with perfect strangers. Oh the dangers, that come along with this self-confidence us Spoken Word Artists display. The opening up of our hearts allowing others to intrude. Defense systems down. Grab the Mic and spit with all your strength and soul so that you might be able to drown out the deafening sound…of nothing.

Silence is the way I determine how you feel. Did I talk too fast? Did they get my message? Did I keep it 100% real?

Because you see Imma poet and I know it. Been Blessed with the gift to formulate rhymes with my words and I won't throw it, away. I even kept writing despite the other kids calling it gay when I would write during my younger years. Embarrassed for even admitting I was writing poetry yet I cried no tears. Partly due to the fact that I was mature beyond my years.

But I learned a valuable lesson then. Something that I've kept and will keep with me until the end. I wasn't writing for the girls or writing to make a friend. I was writing for me. So I never became discouraged because of others doubts and negativity. I just continued to write pursuing my goal of unity. Being able to create a connection, with others who think like I think and un-afraid to show their affection, for other poets and writers of all different kinds.

Unique styles, courageous and thoughtful minds. All cut from a different mold. So we've been told.

But even though at times I've tried to conform to the ideas and concepts that society says is the norm; the overwhelming desire for others to pat me on the back and place me upon a pedestal for the world to see does not interest me. Because I know who I am and when you know who you are you're able to move along through life without the second thoughts about personal decisions in regards to the path you take. At times I've bent a little but I'll never break. And I'm so glad that I was strong enough not to make the mistake of putting away my pen and giving up on the writing. To not pursue my dream is an example to someone else that it's not worth the fighting.

But I'm a Poet and I know it. And I refuse to waste this gift I've been given and just throw it, away. Because too much has been invested to stray from the path based on other's beliefs and ideas that they suggested. And even if there is continued doubt in my ability. I am a Poet and as long as I know it, that's good enough for me.

A LOCKED HEART

Our friendship is rocky
Like the waves in an Angry sea.
As bad as the weather is
There's no place I'd rather be.
Your vision is Blind when it comes to Love
And I'd like to make you see.
You have a Lock around your heart
But you can give the key to me.

DAVID HUNTER JR.

CARE-less THINKING

I THOUGHT I was alone
And then I met you.
I THOUGHT you were perfect
There was no wrong you could do.
When you said that you Loved me
I THOUGHT your heart was true
I know people cheat
I just never THOUGHT it would be you.

UNWANTED TRUTH

You try and hurt with words you have no understanding of. Trying to wear me down with your negativity. It's crazy to remember that I once thought we should be. Pretty eyes with a sour tongue. An overused excuse of "I'm sorry, I was young". Only using emotion and no intellect when you speak. The louder you became, the more easy to see how weak, and fragile you were. These are just some of the reasons I replaced you with her.

No regrets about mistakes of the past. Just a realization that some things aren't meant to last. And now I'm free to take off my heart-shaped cast. Because I'm healed. The Un-wanted truth has now been revealed. When I truly listened I could hear the subtle thoughts of your unconscious mind in your speech. Standing right beside you, I stretched my arms and still could not reach….you…so much potential to become what I aspired for you to be. Dreams of a future that included you + me. But then I awoke, back to reality.

Many questions were asked and I received no reply. Only a kiss on the cheek and a wave goodbye. I was told real love lasts forever but that turned out to be a lie. Because my love for you was deeper than deep and I made a vow to myself that I would forever keep, you…by my side. But now I realize that we can no longer coincide.

Disappointed, with a hint of frustration. Because a kiss on the cheek is no compensation for the end. 1st time this has happened to me and I'm ready to break the trend. But I guess it had to be done. It took me a while to see you weren't the one, and that's cool. I'd rather be happy, young and wise than a bitter, old, fool. Hanging on to the illusion of something that was never real. A non-existent love that still makes me feel, like I was played. I wish you nothing but the best but sometimes I think about what might have been if you had stayed.

GOD I'M SORRY

I'm sorry that I messed up.
I'm sorry for my sins.
I'm sorry that you want to be part of my life
but I don't always let you in.
I'm sorry for sometimes lying.
And I'm sorry for always using the excuse of
"God you know I'm trying".
I'm sorry for all my doubts.
I'm sorry for all my fears.
I'm sorry for falling short of my potential
and your desires for me all these years.
I'm sorry for saying I'm sorry.
I'm sorry for not being a good friend.
And I'm sorry that sometime in the very near future
I'm gonna have to say that I'm sorry again.

MEMORIES OF TOMORROW

After so many ups and downs in my life.
It's a miracle in itself that I'm still in my right mind.
Take a walk in my shoes and there's no doubt that you will find.
It's a miracle in itself that I'm still in my right mind.
And even though I can't forget about yesterday's sorrow.
I just keep looking forward to the Memories of Tomorrow.

AFTER EVERYTHING

On the brink of breakthrough. Riding in Life's car wondering where will it take you? Certain situations may try to break you. But those same situations are the ones that make you. It's time to get back 2 Basics. Like back in the day running track, instead of Nikes we rocked Asics. Music was real with a message for the heart. Families stayed together and hardly were apart.

Too much time being wasted on being upset. It's time to move on, but still not forget. It's ok to remember, those lonely nights in November, when you didn't think you'd make it. Talkin to yourself sayin I just can't take it. It's ok. Everybody feels that way at one time or another. But there's a time to mourn and a time to recover….

And after everything I've been through, I wouldn't have made it without my Mother…

…GOD BLESS HER LIFE…

LOVE IS

Love is hard.
Love is not easy to find and if you're lucky enough to find it you begin to realize how difficult it is to hang on to.
Love is a feeling inside your heart that grows every second that you have it in your possession.
Love is an obsession.
Love is strong, yet it makes us weak for the individual that we Love.
The true definition for Love has no limit to the words that can explain; but a person's name is what we associate it with.
Love is beautiful.
Love is a gift.
Love….hurts.
Especially when we Love and there's no Love given back to us.
Love is amazing.
Love is trust.

Love is unconditional.
Love is a must…in all successful relationships that we desire.
Love is dangerous like a raging fire.
Love….is wack.
Love is broken hearts and never thinking back to that painful memory in your brain.
Love is confusing because all Love is not the same.
Love is genuine.
Love is real.
Love is how those Cheddar Biscuits from Red Lobster make you feel.
Love takes time.
Love is at first sight.
Love is a wedding ring.

Love is the wedding night.
Love is something special and what most of us long to experience in our days of living.
Love is sharing.
Love is giving.
Love is not forced.
Love is a choice.
Love is that feeling you get when you hear that special someone's voice.

Love is not worth the fight.
Love is the best feeling in the world.
Love is a kiss goodnight.
Love is mis-guided.
Love is been there done that. Had some. Tried it.
Love is a game.
Love is overrated.
Love is God
…and the reason that we were created…

"WHILE I'M BEING PATIENT"

Lord, please help me not to become complacent while I'm being patient. You know my heart's desire and the burning fire that exists within my frame. I've prayed about this many times before so there is no shame in saying that I think I've found the one. She's the most beautiful woman I have ever seen. Not just for her looks and style of dress or because her walk is mean. And this prayer that I pray is way more sincere than the prayers I prayed as a teen; when my motives were out of sync with your play. But I come to you tonight hoping and believing that you will understand how I'm feelin.

I was told to trust you with all my heart and soul and life would have no ceiling, for the places I'm tryin to go. So, Lord, continue to sustain me during my time of waiting. Thanking you for your never-ending Grace and Mercy instead of negating, the Blessings that you provide for me every single day. Sometimes my prayers only consist of requests but tonight I humble myself and say...
"From the bottom of my heart, to the depths of my soul...
YES Lord"

Please make me the man that you want me to be. Take away any and everything that will keep me, from reaching my full potential. The waiting game while being single is suspenseful but I'm not resentful, about the others I see; enjoying their partners company. Because I know that there is a specific plan you have for me.

So I will continue to wait and grow. Until you give me the word that it is ok for me to go, and speak words out of my heart to the woman that you have in store. Even if for some reason it's not the woman that I've prayed for. Because God, you know what's best. This waiting period is extremely difficult at times but with you I will pass the test.

And whatever woman you allow into my life will be better than the rest, along with everything I need. I thank you in advance for this Blessing. And with you in my life,
I can't help but to succeed.

NOTHING COMPARES

Many relationships from my past didn't last because I was moving too fast and was unable to grasp the full understanding of what it took to be a real man. But here I am, wiser and more mature. Growing and learning so that when the next woman comes around I'll be sure, to take the time and move a whole lot slower. Time to have a few conversations and *really* get to know her. Be patient and set the tone of what I desire us to be. And hopefully she, will see, that I truly do care enough to make this thing right. **Everything** pleasing in God's sight. No need to argue and fight, about trivial matters or misunderstandings between her and I.

Because in all <u>Honesty,</u> I cannot lie. I'm just not tryna be that guy, who I wanted to be and was before. A brotha who just couldn't ignore, the thrill of the chase. Got with a woman and 1 day later had to replace, her with a new face. Immaturity on display like you had never seen in your life. But no longer is this the situation because I'm searchin for a wife. Remaining patient even though it's not an easy thing to do. Just wanting to make sure I'm making wise decisions in the lady I pursue.

And this is the best choice I've ever made. Playing games with my feelings but became tired of getting played. So slowly I had to fade, away, and stay, in my own lane in order to obtain the woman who would have the honor of taking my last name. And I can't overstate, that all this time has been worth the wait. She loves me and I can't help but to reciprocate, Love back to her. A Love so real and something my lady more than deserves.

There's no real explanation for how this change in my mind occurred, but it is absurd, to know that at one point in my life I acted foolish in my ways for a countless number of days. And I'd like to say that it was just a phase and use the excuse of being young and my hormones feeling like a blaze, of fire. But with this change in my thinking I've been givin my heart's desire.

And there is no greater Love than what I have today. I could take all the women from my past combined and none of them could ever make me feel this way. But the past is the past and the memories of previous women no longer exist. Because nothing compares to the passionate stares of my woman and a relationship such as this.

FOREVER YOURS

A lot of time in my life has been spent with me thinking of you. And you thinking about I. Me wondering if you think that I could ever be **that** guy, in your life. And I'm not talking about your boyfriend or your man. I'm talking about husband and wife. And I must admit that I am different from all those other guys. I never hollered at you callin you "baby" or "boo". And my goal wasn't to get inside your thighs. And ladies this is that time in the poem where I should be hearin some replies, like "Amen" or "Preach". And I know this ain't church so please don't get mad at me. I'm just trying to help you see. That there's really no need for you to waste time, just go ahead and choose me.

There are so many reasons as to why it is you I desire. From the look in your eyes when we speak, to when we first met, those eyes and your smile kinda had me weak. But you would never know it. Only thought in my head was, man, just don't blow it, and say something dumb. I wanted everything to be perfect because I knew that you were the one. And if there is only one word I could use to describe you, it would be Complete. You were the Total Package.

Your sense of fashion. Simply Amazing. Everytime you stepped out in public you had all the fellas craving, for your touch. And I think the word craving might've hyped it a little bit much but you understand what I mean. You were my woman and every other guy's dream. Based just off your looks. But what others didn't know is that money, cars, and flashy clothes are not what it took, to get your attention. And I'd like to say that I already knew this but that would not be true. You were just so beautiful and I had to talk to you.

One conversation turned into 6 years. My heart skipped a few beats when I proposed and you broke down in tears. Even though the chances of you saying no were slim, I still had fear flowing throughout my brain. Just the thought of losing you and things never being the same had me feeling a stressful pain, inside my heart. But your answer was yes so I've never had to worry about that part.

But in reality, things are not the same. And now I truly know what they mean when they say "life is not a game". 6 years, 7 months, 1 day. I'll remember what happened for the rest of my life like it was yesterday.

Making plans for our wedding. Our favorite song on repeat. Taking 5 minute breaks from sending out invitations, to think about how much you complete....me. My cell phone rang. I just listened. Didn't talk. Hung up the phone. Then went for a walk. Hurt, Sad, Angry, Depressed. These are just some of the feelings and emotions that you could use to dress, who I had become. Many people are still searching for the love of their lives but I had already found my One.

    My best friend.

        My lady.

            My lover.

                My future wife.

No longer living because a stray bullet took your life.

I've heard all the cliché's about how God needed another Angel up in Heaven, but that saying don't mean nothing to me because we used the same excuse for my next door neighbor little Kevin. He was only 7. Wrong place, Wrong time. Yeah, Yeah, I've heard that one too. I keep asking God why would He allow someone to harm an Angel? An Angel as special as you. Stray bullets don't have names on them but the people they kill sure do.

So as I look down on your grave. Tears flowing down my cheek. I just wanted to tell you, one more time, that your eyes and smile still make me weak. I am, and will always be...

..…Forever Yours……

MY NAME IS SUCCESS

My name is Success. And I wanted to be with you until the end. But you wouldn't wait, for me. Blinded by the lights and fabricated thoughts of becoming famous dis-abled your ability to see that My name is Success. You and I were destined for each other but you lacked the patience which was needed to become more than those that preceded your existence. So much resistance from the path that was planned for you to take. You closed your ears to the suggestions I would make. And now you say I didn't warn you, but in actuality, I tried.

But instead of listening to me, it was in strangers who you would confide. All because they lied, saying that they were down to ride, along on your journey towards fame. But didn't you hear me when I said that My name….is, Success? Your parents prayed for me to be with you and I vowed that I would forever Bless, everything you would do from now until your end. Yet because of your lack of wisdom we didn't even get to begin.

My words are not meant to break you. But they do serve as a reminder as to where I was going to take you. Oh what could have been if you had allowed me to make you; into the star you were destined to become. People still speak highly of you nowadays but you could've been the 1!

The whole inside your soul continues to grow with every breath you breathe. Your parents are gone. So-called friends have moved on. Yet still for some reason you don't believe that My name is Success! And all I wanted for you was the best.

It's easy for you to sit here now and write about all the things that went wrong. Count the mistakes that have been made and sing the same old sad song of "Why Me?". But when it comes to singing that song, you're not the first. Many others before you had a chance to be with me as well and instead they chose the thirst; of riches, fame and glory. So many different people who all share the same story about how much I loved them so. Yet they chose to ignore my advances. Thus throwing away all their chances of a future between them and I.

If you would have just waited patiently for me, I was going to open your eyes to how successful you could be. But the pressure of the crowd became too loud. It corrupted your mind as you wasted your time and it raised your level of stress. A painful lesson learned about the opportunities that were spurned because you did not choose me…. Success.

A WALKING TESTIMONY

"Somebody Prayed for me. They had me on their mind. They took the time to pray for me. I'm so glad they prayed. I'm so glad they prayed. I'm so glad they prayed for me."

I know this is supposed to be a poem so I don't mean to bore you. But I am a Walking Testimony standing right here before you. You see last year I became extremely sick in my body. Felt as if I were left for dead. I stayed up all night on the computer, googling everything that the Doctor said. I was tryna figure out some things. I even started having trouble breathing. Called my Mother up and she told me to get off that computer and to stop all that reading. So I just asked her if she would pray for me; and without hesitation, she did.

You see, it was already humbling for me to know that in my weakest hour somebody that I knew got down on their knees, prayed a prayer, and, cried for me. But I was the one breaking down into tears when thinking about how Jesus and I never physically met but He got up on a cross and, died for me. Sacrificing His life, for my sin. Thus automatically claiming the title of my Savior and forever my best friend. And yes that's exactly how I wanted this poem to start and begin. A poetic expression. That some might describe as a 3 minute and 22 second confession about how my life has been changed all because….

"Somebody prayed for me…"

Hands clasped together. Pointed up towards the sky. Tears rolling down their face praying "please don't let him die"...

"They had me on their mind…"

Not worried about themselves. Their only thoughts focusing on the details of my pain. Excited and encouraged with every ounce of strength I continued to gain.

"They took the time to pray for me…."

Never mind the fact that I was in the hospital. Consumed by fear and a paralyzing type of stress. Over 40lbs lost in less than 2 months so you could say that I was a mess.

"But I'm so glad they prayed…"

Because without their prayers I know I wouldn't be here today. No longer taking anything for granted because I ain't got time to play.

"And I'm so glad they prayed…."

Sowing a seed on my behalf. Praying and believing that I would recover. My head's held high towards Heaven knowing God did it and it couldn't have been any other. And that's why…

"I'm so glad they prayed…

…for…

…me"

ACKNOWLEDGMENTS

First and foremost I would like to thank God for Blessing me with the ability and opportunity to write this book. The inspiration that was given to me has truly enhanced the quality of "Pen In My Hand" and the material that is included.

I am Blessed to have very special parents who have given me guidance and shared their wisdom with me throughout the years. Without their help I would not be who I am today.

Individually I want to thank My Mother for a special reason. It was the idea that God placed upon your heart to turn these writings into a book that should be published and shared with the world. You have encouraged me more than you know and because of your support, I kept pushing even when I did not think I could continue. The vision that you shared with me has now transformed into a reality and for that, I will be forever grateful.

To my Father, there aren't enough words to say about how I feel so I'll just say thank you for being such a great example of what a Real Man should be. I have watched you over the years and listened intently to your instruction and because of you I am better.

To my friend Yurri Mial, I thank you sir for your incredible work and vision when it came to making the design for my book cover. Everyone that sees the book design simply raves about it and asks me if I was the one who drew it or came up with the design and that is a tribute to your fine work. I appreciate you and I know that you are on your way to accomplishing great things in life and in your field.

To my brother, Daniel K. Hunter, who listened and critiqued my poems along with my spoken word performances, I thank you. Your critiques, both positive and negative, allowed me to word the writings so that everyone would comprehend every single sentence I read and spoke. You have made me a better writer and an even better performer because of your honesty and willingness to assist me in going above and beyond what I thought I could be as a writer. It is an honor to have a brother like you.

DAVID HUNTER JR.

To my friend and Manager, Tatiana M. Johnson, I cannot thank you enough for everything that you've done. Helping me put this entire project together along with helping me to market this book and finalize everything in a professional manner is something I am so thankful for. Going out of your way to have late night meetings and discussions on various topics along with your insight to this project allowed it to reach its full potential.

All of the support shown to me has been greatly appreciated. It keeps me going and helps me stay encouraged throughout each and every day. Without a good support system, you are nothing. I have been Blessed to meet and know so many great people who have always shown me Love and for that I am truly thankful.

Sincerely,

David Hunter Jr.   "DJ"

AFTERWORD

To my dear and strong son, DJ-

Pen in my Hand is a written work of art. It is inspiring and insightful, truthful and witty, sometimes real and raw and oft-times pretty and even "preachy". You have taken a pen and in your hand have created provoking poems, including "Deeper and Deeper", "If I could just Believe", "Poetic Politics", "Special Bond" and the especially insightful "To My Daughter". The flow of maturity that takes us on a journey from the first lines of "My Life Story" to the "Memories of Tomorrow" is indeed profound.

You prayed that I would be proud of you and I am more than proud of you; I am blessed with a son who continues to grow and bloom into a man who is an example to and for other young men to follow. I am proud of you more for who you are than for what you have done. And what you have done is worth reading and sharing. On this Independence Day, I celebrate you and how you have honored your parents and depended on God.

Your loving father,

Dad

July 4th, 2011

DAVID HUNTER JR.

FOR BOOKING & SPEAKING INQUIRIES

1st Lady Management

Talent Management

Office: (818) 925.LADY (5239)

Email: Tmj@1stladymanagement.com

Made in the USA
Charleston, SC
29 June 2013